Sugar-Free Cakes Muffins and Tarts

40 Amazing Recipes

by

Elizabeth Gordon

Disclaimer

Copyright © December 2014 **Sugar-Free Cakes, Cookies, Muffins and Tarts 40 Amazing Recipes**
 by Elizabeth Gordon

FOR EXCELLENT FREE and 99 CENTS BOOKS from AMAZON, NOOK, KOBO, SMASHWORDS etc TRY BUCK BOOKs

buckbooks.net/2618.html

You may also enjoy:

HOROSCOPE 2015: Astrology and Numerology Horoscopes – lisa Lazuli

The mystery/thrillers:

A Sealed Fate – Lisa Gordon

Holly Leaves – Lisa Gordon

Next of Sin – Lisa Gordon

As well as (all in ebook and paperback):

Delicious, Nutritious Recipes for the Time and Cash Strapped – Lisa Lazuli

Paleo Diet: Get Started, Get Motivated, Feel Great. – BESTSELLER – Elizabeth Gordon

99 ACE Places to Promote Your Book – Lisa lazuli

Pressure Cooking Reinvented. – BEST SELLER – Lisa Lazuli

SUGAR FREE DESSERTS WITH PAZAZ – NEW – Lisa Lazuli

Weight Loss with the Nordic Diet – NEW – Saga Finberg

Be Wine Savvy – BESTSELLER – Joelle Nevin

Contents

Introduction..7

Cakes 9

No Sugar Applesauce Cake...9

Blueberry Crumble Cake..11

Mocha Cake 13

Grated Apple Cake 14

Spiced Carrot Cake 15

Banana Chocolate Chip Cake 17

Lemon Poppy Seed Sugar-Free Cake 18

Sliced Almond Chocolate Cake 19

Hazelnut Loaf Cake...21

Sticky Date Cake..23

Cookies 25

Peanut Butter Cookies..25

Chocolate Chip Sugar-Free Cookies.................................26

Brandy Raisin Oatmeal Cookies 27

Chewy Chocolate Cookies..28

Ginger Crisp Cookies...29

Pear Cookies...30

Lavender Shortbread Cookies...31

Coconut Cookies..32

Gingerbread Cookies 33

Breakfast Cranberry Cookies 35

Pies and Tarts 37

Ginger Pumpkin Pie 37

Mango Curd Tart..39

Berry Cherry No Crust Pie 41

No Crust Pumpkin Pie 42

Coconut Lemon Curd Tart 43

Walnut Apple Pie 45

Sweet Potato Pie 47

Fresh Berry Mint Tart 49

Sugar-Free Pear Pie 51

Peanut Butter Smooth Pie 53

Muffins **55**

Banana Blueberry Muffins 55

Everything-but-the-kitchen-sink Muffins 56

Sugar-Free Pumpkin Muffins 57

Raspberry Whole Wheat Muffins 58

Banana Peanut Butter Muffins 59

Sugar-Free Carrot Muffins 60

Nectarine Pecan Muffins 61

Plum Bran Muffins 62

Zucchini Quinoa Muffins 63

Chocolate Zucchini Muffins 65

Conclusion 67

Introduction

The amount of sugar found in food nowadays is staggering! If we were to compare our diet today and the diet of our ancestors the conclusion would be that we consume dozens of times more sugar. But while this has changed since ancient times, our bodies remained the same this whole time. Our bodies have been processing food the exact same way for thousands of years, but if thousands of years ago our system only had to deal with fruits, vegetables and meat, it now has to deal with incredibly large amounts of sugar and other additives that often come with it in the form of great looking and tasty desserts and sweet treats.

In these conditions, there is no wonder that often our system fails and it breaks into what doctors consider the diseases of the century – type II diabetes, obesity and heart problems. All these come as a package once your body struggles to process food properly. Once obesity is installed, type II diabetes moves in shortly too, making plenty of room for heart problems – the most dangerous trio, experts say!

Luckily, more and more people are concerned about what they eat and a new trend has risen in the last few years – sugar-free foods. This trend seems to have two tendencies: either replacing the sugar with a healthier sweetener or cutting off the refined sugar completely and relying on natural sources of sweetener, such as fruits and nuts. Moreover, these foods also include healthier ingredients, such as whole wheat flour, oats, quinoa, fresh fruits, nuts or dates so they are not only sugar-free, but also healthier, have more nutrients and provide you with the needed energy in the form of healthy carbs and not refined carbs coming from refined sugar.

This book focuses mostly on desserts that have no refined sugar added and most recipes in fact don't require any other processed sweetener either. Instead, the place of the sweetener has been taken by healthy additions, fresh fruits or interesting flavor combinations so those of you who give these recipes a try have nothing to lose, but to gain! 40 decadent sugar-free recipes, from cakes to cookies, pies and muffins are at your disposal so you don't have to reach for that bar of chocolate or that candy next time you crave for something sweet. Simply bake yourself a batch of these and snack on desserts that are both delicious and healthy!

Cakes

No Sugar Applesauce Cake

This recipe replaces the sugar with the natural sweetness of the applesauce and it manages to deliver a delicious, moist cake that tastes like a piece of autumn with its numerous spices.

Time: 1 hour
Servings: 10

Ingredients:
2 cups all-purpose flour
1 pinch salt
1 teaspoon baking powder
1 teaspoon baking soda
1/2 teaspoon cinnamon powder
1/2 teaspoon ground ginger
1 pinch nutmeg
1 1/2 cups applesauce
1/4 cup vegetable oil
3 eggs
1 teaspoon vanilla extract
2 green apples, peeled, cored and sliced
1/4 cup raisins

Directions:
1. Preheat your oven to 350F and line a round cake pan with baking paper. Place it aside until needed.
2. Sift the flour with salt, baking powder, baking soda, cinnamon, ginger and nutmeg in a bowl.
3. In a different bowl, mix the applesauce with eggs, oil and vanilla. Stir in the dry ingredients then fold in the apples and raisins.
4. Pour the batter into your pan and bake in the oven for 40 minutes or until a toothpick inserted in the center of the cake comes out clean.

5. Allow the cake to cool in the pan before placing on a platter and serving.

Blueberry Crumble Cake

The highlight of this cake is the crisp topping which creates a delicious contrast with the delicate sponge and blueberries.

Time: 1 hour
Servings: 10

Ingredients:
Cake:
3/4 cup butter, melted and chilled
1 cup whole milk
4 cggs
1 teaspoon vanilla extract
2 ripe bananas, mashed
3 cups all-purpose flour
2 teaspoons baking powder
1 pinch salt
1/2 cup fresh or frozen blueberries
Topping:
1/2 cup all-purpose flour
1/4 cup butter, chilled and cubed
1 pinch salt
1/4 cup rolled oats

Directions:
1. Preheat your oven to 350F and line a round cake pan with parchment paper. Place it aside until the batter is done.
2. For the cake, mix the butter, milk, eggs, vanilla and bananas in a bowl.
3. Stir in the flour, baking powder and salt and give it a quick mix. Fold in the blueberries then pour the batter into your prepared pan.
4. For the topping, mix all the ingredients in a bowl and rub them together with a fork until grainy.
5. Spread the topping over the cake then place the cake in the oven and bake for 40 minutes or until well risen, golden brown and crisp.

6. Allow the cake to cool on a wire rack before slicing.

Mocha Cake

This mocha cake is a treat for any dessert lover. The coffee taste is not overpowering at all since the recipe manages to balance the amount of ingredients used well.

Time: 1 hour
Servings: 8

Ingredients:
3/4 cup freshly brewed coffee
1/2 cup butter, melted
4 drops Stevia
1 egg
1 teaspoon vanilla extract
1 1/2 cups all-purpose flour
1 pinch salt
1/3 cup cocoa powder
1 teaspoon baking powder
1 teaspoon baking soda
1/2 cup walnuts, chopped

Directions:
1. Preheat your oven to 350F and line a baking pan with parchment paper or grease it with butter.
2. Combine the coffee, butter, stevia, egg and vanilla in a bowl then stir in the flour, salt, cocoa powder, baking powder, baking soda and give it a good mix.
3. Fold in the walnuts then pour the batter into your prepared pan and bake in the oven for 40-45 minutes or until well risen and golden brown. To check if the cake is done, insert a toothpick in the center of the cake – if the cake is done, the toothpick comes out clean. If the toothpick comes out with traces of batter, bake the cake a few more minutes and check again.
4. Let the cake cool on a wire rack before slicing and serving.

Grated Apple Cake

The moisture of this cake is given by its main ingredient – grated apples. Combined with cinnamon, ginger and nutmeg, plus walnuts for texture, the recipe yields a delicious cake with a delicate crunch.

Time: 1 1/4 hours
Servings: 8-10

Ingredients:
1 1/4 cups all-purpose flour
1 pinch salt
1 teaspoon baking powder
1/2 teaspoon baking soda
1/2 cup butter
1 teaspoon cinnamon powder
1 teaspoon orange zest
3 eggs
1 1/2 cups grated apples
1/4 cup applesauce
1/2 cup walnuts, chopped
1/2 cup raisins

Directions:
1. Mix the butter with cinnamon and orange zest in a bowl then add the eggs, one by one.
2. Stir in the apples and applesauce then fold in the flour sifted with salt and baking powder and baking soda.
3. Add the walnuts and raisins and pour the batter into a round cake pan lined with parchment paper.
4. Bake the cake in the preheated oven at 350F for 40-45 minutes or until well risen and golden brown.
5. Allow the cake to cool in the pan or on a wire rack before slicing.

Spiced Carrot Cake

Carrot cake is a classic, no doubt about that! It never ceases to impress with its texture and spiced taste. And here is a recipe that doesn't ask for sugar, relying on the natural sweetness of the carrots.

Time: 1 hour
Servings: 8

Ingredients:
Cake:
1 cup all-purpose flour
1 teaspoon cinnamon powder
1 teaspoon ground ginger
1 teaspoon baking soda
3 eggs
1 teaspoon vanilla extract
1/2 cup vegetable oil
1 1/2 cups grated carrots
1/4 cup raisins
Topping:
1 cup cream cheese, softened
1/4 cup butter, room temperature
2 tablespoons stevia powder

Directions:
1. Preheat your oven to 350F and line a round cake pan with parchment paper.
2. To make the cake, sift the flour with cinnamon, ginger and baking soda and place them aside.
3. Mix the eggs for 5 minutes, until fluffy. Stir in the vanilla and oil and mix well.
4. Fold in carrots and raisins then pour the batter into your prepared cake pan and bake for 40-45 minutes or until golden brown and risen.
5. Allow the cake to cool on a wire rack while you prepare the frosting.

6. For the frosting, mix the cream cheese, butter and stevia in a bowl.
7. Spread the frosting over the cake once it's chilled.
8. Serve the cake chilled.

Banana Chocolate Chip Cake

Banana and chocolate are a match made in heaven and this cake is the proof of that. The bananas have not only a delicate aroma, but also a special natural sweetness which enriches the cake perfectly.

Time: 1 hour
Servings: 8-10

Ingredients:
2 cups all-purpose flour
1 pinch salt
1 teaspoon cinnamon powder
1 pinch nutmeg
1 teaspoon baking powder
1/2 teaspoon baking soda
3/4 cup whole milk
2 eggs
2 ripe bananas, mashed
1/4 cup vegetable oil
1 teaspoon vanilla extract
1/2 cup dark chocolate chips

Directions:
1. Preheat your oven to 350F and line a round cake pan with parchment paper, placing the pan aside until needed.
2. Combine the flour, salt, cinnamon, nutmeg, baking powder and baking soda in a bowl and mix well.
3. Mix the rest of the ingredients, except the chocolate chips, in a different bowl and give them a good mix then fold in the flour and mix gently with a spatula until incorporated.
4. Add the chocolate chips and pour the batter into your pan.
5. Bake in the oven for 40, up to 45 minutes or until golden brown and well risen.
6. Cool the cake on a wire rack before slicing and serving.

Lemon Poppy Seed Sugar-Free Cake

The mix between lemon and poppy seeds is a classic and it never ceases to impress due to the contrast created by the tangy and fragrant lemon and the crunchy, slightly bitter poppy seeds.

Time: 1 hour
Servings: 6-8

Ingredients
1 cup all-purpose flour
2 tablespoons poppy seeds
1 teaspoon baking powder
1 teaspoon baking soda
1 pinch salt
4 drops stevia
2 egg yolks
2 eggs
2 tablespoons vegetable oil
1/3 cup plain yogurt
2 tablespoons lemon juice
2 teaspoons lemon zest

Directions:
1. Preheat your oven to 350F and line a round cake pan with parchment paper, placing it aside until needed.
2. Combine the flour, poppy seeds, baking powder, baking soda and salt in a bowl.
3. In a different bowl, mix the stevia with egg yolks and eggs until fluffy.
4. Add the oil, yogurt, lemon juice and lemon zest and mix well then fold in the flour using a spatula.
5. Pour the batter into your prepared pan and bake in the oven for 40 minutes or until golden brown and well risen and fragrant.
6. Allow the cake to cool in the pan for 10 minutes then transfer on a cooling rack to cool completely.

Sliced Almond Chocolate Cake

This cake is loaded with chocolate and absolutely delicious with its crunchy, delicate almond topping. Just a slice is enough to make your taste buds happy!

Time: 1 hour
Servings: 6-8

Ingredients:
3 egg whites
1 pinch salt
1/2 teaspoon lemon juice
4 drops stevia extract
2/3 cup whole milk
1 cup all-purpose flour
1/4 cup dark cocoa powder
1/2 teaspoon baking soda
1/4 teaspoon baking powder
1/2 cup sliced almonds

Directions:
1. Preheat your oven to 350F and line a round cake pan with parchment paper.
2. Sift the flour with cocoa powder, baking soda and baking powder.
3. Combine the egg whites with salt and lemon juice and mix them until stiff.
4. Add the stevia, mixing until well combined and the mixture becomes glossy and stiff, at least 5 minutes.
5. Fold in the cocoa mixture, alternating it with milk.
6. Pour the batter into your pan and top with sliced almonds.
7. Bake in the oven for 35-40 minutes or until well risen and the top is golden brown.
8. When done, remove the cake from the oven and turning upside down to prevent it from deflating completely.
9. Once chilled, transfer it on a platter and slice.

Hazelnut Loaf Cake

Loaf cakes are easier to store than regular cakes since they can easily be wrapped in baking paper and placed in a bag to keep fresh for a longer period of time. Plus, they are versatile and many variations can be made using one basic recipe. This particular recipe is one of those examples, but changes can still be made with a bit of imagination.

Time: 1 hour
Servings: 8-10

Ingredients:
1 1/3 cups all-purpose flour
1/4 cup rolled oats
1 cup hazelnuts, divided
1/4 teaspoon cinnamon powder
1 pinch salt
1 teaspoon baking powder
1/2 teaspoon baking soda
1/2 cup sour cream
2 eggs
1/4 cup vegetable oil
1 teaspoon vanilla extract

Directions:
1. Preheat your oven to 350F and grease a loaf pan with butter.
2. Combine the flour, oats, half of the hazelnuts, cinnamon, salt, baking powder and baking soda in a food processor and pulse until ground.
3. Stir in the sour cream, eggs, oil and vanilla and pulse just until mixed.
4. Pour the batter into your loaf pan and top with the remaining hazelnuts, slightly chopped.
5. Bake in the oven for 40-45 minutes or until golden brown and well risen.
6. When done, remove the cake from the oven and transfer it on a wire rack to cool.

7. Serve it chilled.

Sticky Date Cake

Similar to the famous sticky toffee pudding, this cake uses dates as the main ingredient and relies on their sweetness and delicate aroma to create a delicious, moist dessert for the entire family.

Time: 1 hour
Servings: 6-8

Ingredients:
1 cup warm water
1 cup dates, pitted
1 pinch salt
1 cup applesauce
1 teaspoon vanilla extract
2 eggs
1/4 cup vegetable oil
2 tablespoons stevia powder
1 1/2 cups all-purpose flour
1 teaspoon baking powder
1/2 teaspoon baking soda
1/2 teaspoon cinnamon powder
1/2 teaspoon ground cardamom

Directions:
1. Preheat your oven to 350F and grease a round cake pan with butter.
2. Combine the water and dates in a blender and pulse until smooth. Spread half of this mixture at the bottom of the cake pan and pour the remaining half in a bowl.
3. Stir in the salt, applesauce, vanilla, eggs and oil and give it a good mix then add the stevia, flour, baking soda, baking powder, cinnamon and cardamom and mix until incorporated.
4. Pour the batter into the pan, over the date mixture and bake in the oven for 40 minutes or until golden brown and fragrant.
5. Allow the cake to cool in the pan before serving.

Cookies

Peanut Butter Cookies

With just 3 ingredients, these cookies are a delight for your taste buds. If you're a peanut butter fan, don't hesitate and make them today!

Time: 40 minutes
Servings: 10

Ingredients:
1 cup smooth peanut butter
1/2 cup stevia powder
1 egg
1/2 teaspoon vanilla extract

Directions:
1. Line a square pan with parchment paper and place it aside. Preheat your oven to 350F.
2. Combine all the ingredients in a bowl and mix well.
3. Drop spoonfuls of batter onto your prepared pan, leaving room between each cookie as they tend to rise and spread slightly.
4. Bake in the oven for 15-17 minutes or until golden brown and fragrant.
5. Don't over-bake them as they tend to dry too much.
6. Let them cool in the pan before serving and store them in an airtight container for up to 1 week.

Chocolate Chip Sugar-Free Cookies

Cookies are not rocket science to bake, that's for sure, but things can get more difficult when it comes to sugar-free cookies as often the balance it hard to get. But worry not as now you have this recipe which is just perfect the way it is!

Time: 40 minutes
Servings: 2 dozen

Ingredients:
2/3 cup butter, softened
4 drops stevia extract
1 teaspoon vanilla extract
2 eggs
1 1/2 cups all-purpose flour
1 teaspoon baking soda
1 pinch salt
1/2 cup dark chocolate chips

Directions:
1. Preheat your oven to 350F and line two baking sheets with baking paper, placing them aside until needed.
2. Combine the butter and stevia in a bowl and mix them for 3 minutes until fluffy. Add the vanilla and eggs and mix well.
3. Fold in the flour, baking soda, salt and chocolate chips.
4. Drop spoonfuls of batter onto your prepared baking sheets and bake for 15-20 minutes or until the edges begin to turn golden brown.
5. When done, remove from the oven and allow the cakes to cool completely before serving or storing them away.

Brandy Raisin Oatmeal Cookies

The title of the recipe says it all! This recipe combines the chewy oats with brandy infused raisins, thus creating some chewy, delicious, fragrant cookies, perfect for the holiday season or just a treat at any time of the year if you want.

Time: 2 hours
Servings: 3 dozen

Ingredients:
1 cup all-purpose flour
2 cups rolled oats
1 teaspoon baking soda
1 teaspoon cinnamon powder
1 pinch salt
2 ripe bananas, mashed
2 eggs
1/2 teaspoon vanilla extract
1/2 cup vegetable oil
1 cup raisins
1/2 cup Brandy

Directions:
1. Combine the raisins with Brandy and let them soak at least 1 hour.
2. Combine the flour, oats, baking soda, cinnamon powder and salt in a bowl.
3. In a different bowl, combine the eggs with bananas and mix until stiff and fluffy.
4. Add the vanilla extract and oil then fold in the flour mixture, followed by the raisins.
5. Drop spoonfuls of mixture on a few baking sheets lined with parchment paper and bake in the preheated oven at 350F for 15-17 minutes or until the edges of the cookies begin to turn golden brown.
6. Let the cookies cool in pan before serving or storing.

Chewy Chocolate Cookies

Two main ingredients make these cookies a real treat for every chocoholic who likes to keep a healthy diet as well and these ingredients are chocolate and oats. Unlike what you might think, they combine well and taste great together.

Time: 40 minutes
Servings: 3 dozen

Ingredients:
1 cup all-purpose flour
1 1/2 cups rolled oats
1/2 cup cocoa powder
1 teaspoon baking powder
1 pinch salt
1/4 cup almond slices
1/4 cup golden raisins
1/2 cup butter, softened
2 tablespoons stevia powder
2 eggs
1 teaspoon vanilla extract

Directions:
1. Preheat your oven to 350F and line 2-3 baking sheets with parchment paper, placing them aside until you're going to need them.
2. Mix the flour, oats, cocoa powder, baking powder, salt, almond slices and raisins in a bowl.
3. In a different bowl, combine the butter and stevia and mix well until smooth. Stir in the eggs and vanilla and give it a good mix.
4. Stir in the flour mixture, spoon by spoon until the batter is well mixed.
5. Drop spoonfuls of batter on your prepared baking sheets and bake for 15-17 minutes or until golden brown.
6. Allow the cookies to cool in the pan before serving or storing in an airtight container for up to 1 week.

Ginger Crisp Cookies

Also known as gingersnaps, these cookies are a Christmas staple with their intense aroma and crisp texture. The ginger flavor, even though intense, it's not overpowering for your taste buds, but it's enough to awaken them.

Time: 45 minutes
Servings: 3 dozen

Ingredients:
1/2 cup butter, softened
4 drops stevia extract
1/4 cup vegetable oil
2 eggs
3 cups all-purpose flour
2 teaspoons baking soda
1/2 teaspoon cinnamon powder
1 1/2 teaspoons ground ginger
1 pinch salt
1 pinch nutmeg

Directions:
1. Mix the butter in a bowl until smooth and creamy, as well as fluffy. Add the stevia extract.
2. Stir in the oil then add the eggs and give it a good mix.
3. Stir in the flour, baking soda, cinnamon, ginger, salt and nutmeg.
4. Give it a quick mix just until well combined then drop spoonfuls of batter on 2-3 baking sheets lined with parchment paper.
5. Bake in the preheated oven at 350F for 15-17 minutes or until the surface of the cookies is crusty, but the inside is still soft.
6. Let the cookies cool completely before serving.

Pear Cookies

These cookies step out of the true meaning of a cookie with the fact that they are moister and slightly chewy, not crisp. But they are delicious nonetheless, especially since they use the delicate and fragrant pears as their main flavor.

Time: 45 minutes
Servings: 3 dozen

Ingredients:
3/4 cup butter, softened
1 teaspoon orange zest
2 eggs
1 teaspoon vanilla extract
1/2 cup applesauce
1/4 cup fresh orange juice
1 1/2 cups all-purpose flour
1 cup rolled oats
1 teaspoon baking soda
1/2 teaspoon baking powder
1/4 teaspoon cinnamon powder
2 ripe pears, peeled and diced

Directions:
1. Preheat your oven to 350F and line 2-3 baking pans with parchment paper.
2. Combine the butter and orange zest in a bowl and mix for 5 minutes until creamy and fluffy.
3. Stir in the eggs, followed by the applesauce and orange juice and mix well.
4. Stir in the flour, oats, baking soda, baking powder and cinnamon then fold in the pears.
5. Drop spoonfuls of batter on your prepared baking pans and bake for 15-20 minutes or until golden brown on the edges.
6. When done, remove from the oven and cool the cookies on wire racks.
7. Store them in an airtight container for up to 4 days.

Lavender Shortbread Cookies

Perfect for any moment of the day or year, these lavender cookies are crisp and fragrant. A touch of lemon zest balances the lavender perfectly so it's not overpowering nor it tastes weird.

Time: 1 hour
Servings: 2 dozen

Ingredients:
1/2 cup butter, softened
1 egg
1 teaspoon lemon zest
1 teaspoon vanilla extract
1 teaspoon lavender flowers
2 1/2 cups all-purpose flour
1 pinch salt
1/2 cup cold milk

Directions:
1. Mix the butter until smooth and fluffy.
2. Stir in the egg, lemon zest, vanilla and lavender flowers, as well as milk then add the flour and salt and mix well.
3. Knead the dough a few times and wrap it well in plastic wrap. Refrigerate for 20 minutes then transfer it on a floured working surface.
4. Roll the dough into a thin sheet and cut into small cookies with a cookie cutter.
5. Transfer the cookies on your baking sheets, lined with parchment paper.
6. Bake in the preheated oven at 350F for 15 minutes or until the edges turn slightly golden brown.
7. Let the cookies cool in the pan before serving.

Coconut Cookies

If you like the delicate aroma of coconut, these cookies are for you. Not only they taste great, but they also are crisp and easy to make. So put your apron on and get baking!

Time: 50 minutes
Servings: 3 dozen

Ingredients:
1/2 cup butter, softened
1 cup all-purpose flour
2 eggs
1 teaspoon vanilla extract
1/2 teaspoon baking powder
1 1/2 cups shredded coconut
1/2 cup chopped almonds

Directions:
1. Preheat your oven to 350F and line 3 baking sheets with parchment paper.
2. Combine the butter, flour, eggs, vanilla and baking powder in a food processor and pulse until smooth.
3. Stir in the coconut and almonds then drop spoonfuls of batter on your prepared baking sheets.
4. Bake in the oven for 15-18 minutes or until the edges of the cookies begin to turn golden brown.
5. Allow the cookies to cool completely in the pan then transfer them in an airtight container to store for up to 1 week.

Gingerbread Cookies

Gingerbread cookies are a Christmas staple in many countries all over the globe and the truth is what would the holidays be without these fragrant, spiced, crispy cookies?! They bring spices into the cold season and announce the holidays at the same time.

Time: 1 1/2 hours
Servings: 2 dozen

Ingredients:
3/4 cup butter, room temperature
4 drops stevia extract
2 eggs
2 cups all-purpose flour
1 teaspoon baking soda
1 tablespoon ground ginger
1 teaspoon cinnamon powder
1/2 teaspoon cocoa powder
1 pinch ground black pepper
1 pinch salt

Directions:
1. Combine the butter and stevia in a bowl and mix well until creamy and smooth, about 2 minutes.
2. Stir in the eggs, one by one, followed by the flours, sifted with baking soda, ginger, cinnamon, cocoa powder, pepper and salt.
3. Knead the dough a few times then wrap it in plastic wrap and refrigerate for 1 hour.
4. Transfer the dough on a floured working surface and roll it into a thin sheet, about 1/4-inch thickness.
5. Using cookies cutter, included gingerbread men, cut small cookies and place them on baking trays lined with parchment paper.
6. Bake in the preheated oven at 350F for 15-20 minutes or until crisp and fragrant.

7. When done, let the cookies cool in the pan before serving or storing in a cookie jar.

Breakfast Cranberry Cookies

These cookies are as healthy as they can be with their addition of cranberries, almonds and rolled oats. Thanks to their high content of fibers, they will keep you full over the day and provide you with the needed nutrients to start the day on a high note.

Time: 50 minutes
Servings: 3 dozen

Ingredients:
1/2 cup butter, softened
2 eggs
2 tablespoons vegetable oil
1 teaspoon vanilla extract
1 cup rolled oats
1 cup all-purpose flour
1 teaspoon baking soda
1 pinch salt
1/2 cup dried cranberries
1/2 cup almonds, chopped

Directions:
1. Mix the in a bowl until creamy and fluffy.
2. Stir in the eggs, one by one, followed by the oil and vanilla extract.
3. Stir in the oats, flour, baking soda and salt.
4. Fold in the cranberries and almonds then drop spoonfuls of batter on your baking sheets lined with parchment paper.
5. Bake in the oven for 15 minutes or until slightly golden brown.
6. Let the cookies cool completely before serving or storing in a cookie jar.

Pies and Tarts

Ginger Pumpkin Pie

Having just a touch of ginger, this pie is delicious and fragrant, as well as creamy and rich. The pecan crust is the perfect match for the ginger pumpkin filling.

Time: 1 1/4 hours
Servings: 8

Ingredients:
Crust:
1/2 cup butter, cold and cubed
1 cup all-purpose flour
1/2 cup ground pecans
1 pinch salt
2 tablespoons cold water
Filling:
1 can pumpkin puree
2 eggs
1 teaspoon cinnamon powder
1 teaspoon ground ginger
1 cup evaporated milk
1 teaspoon stevia extract
1 pinch salt

Directions:
1. Preheat your oven to 350F and prepare a round pie pan.
2. To make the crust, mix all the ingredients in a food processor and pulse until a dough forms.
3. Transfer the dough on a floured working surface and roll it into a thin sheet.
4. Transfer the dough into your prepared pan and press it well on the bottom and sides of the pan.
5. For the filling, mix all the ingredients in a bowl.

6. Pour the filling into the crust and bake in the oven for 40-45 minutes or until the edges are slightly golden brown and crisp and the center looks set.
7. Let the pie cool completely before slicing and serving.

Mango Curd Tart

If you ever made lemon curd, this mango curd will be piece of cake to master. The principles of making it are the same, but the taste is much milder and it has a natural sweetness that doesn't need any sweetener additions.

Time: 1 1/2 hours
Servings: 8

Ingredients:
Crust:
1 cup ground almonds
1/2 cup all-purpose flour
2 tablespoons butter, melted
1 pinch salt
Filling:
3 ripe mango, peeled and cubed
1/2 cup butter, cubed
1 teaspoon lemon juice
4 egg yolks
Topping:
1 cup coconut cream, whipped

Directions:
1. To make the crust, combine all the ingredients in a food processor and pulse until well combined.
2. Transfer the mixture into a tart pan and press it well on the bottom and sides of the pan.
3. Bake in the preheated oven at 350F for 10-15 minutes then remove from the oven and let it cool completely.
4. For the filling, mix the mango cubes and lemon juice in a food processor.
5. Transfer the mango puree in a heatproof bowl and stir in the egg yolks and butter.
6. Place the bowl over a hot water bath and cook for 20 minutes until it begins to thicken slightly.
7. Remove from heat and allow the curd to cool completely.

8. Spoon the curd into the tart crust and top with whipped coconut cream.
9. Refrigerate until the serving time.

Berry Cherry No Crust Pie

Fragrant and juicy, this pie is the proof that fruit desserts are the best when it comes to reducing the sugar in your diet. The berries and cherries are both sweet enough to be eaten without additional sweetener, just give it a try!

Time: 1 1/4 hours
Servings: 8

Ingredients:
2 cups fresh or frozen berries
2 cups fresh or frozen cherries, pitted
2 tablespoons cornstarch
1 cup rolled oats
1/2 cup all-purpose flour
1/2 cup almond flour
1/2 cup butter, cubed
1 pinch salt

Directions:
1. Preheat your oven to 350F and slightly grease a deep baking pan with butter.
2. Mix the berries, cherries and cornstarch in your prepared pan.
3. For the topping, mix the oats, flour, almond flour, salt and butter in a bowl and rub them together until grainy.
4. Spread this mixture over the fruits and bake in the oven for 30-40 minutes or until golden brown and crusty on top.
5. Serve the pie slightly warm or chilled.

No Crust Pumpkin Pie

Unlike a traditional pie, this recipe has no crust. And yet, the final pie holds its shape well and it's easy to slice but just as creamy and delicious as a traditional pie. What's not to love about it?!

Time: 1 hour
Servings: 8

Ingredients:
1 can pumpkin puree
4 eggs
1 teaspoon cinnamon powder
1 cup evaporated milk
1 pinch salt
1 teaspoon vanilla extract
4 drops stevia extract
1/2 cup almond flour
2 tablespoons cornstarch
Butter to grease the pan

Directions:
1. Preheat your oven to 330F and grease a round pie pan with butter.
2. Combine the pumpkin puree with the rest of the ingredients in a food processor or blender and pulse until smooth and creamy.
3. Pour the mixture into your prepared pan and bake in the oven for 45 minutes or until the center of the pie looks set.
4. Allow the pie to cool in the pan before slicing and serving.

Coconut Lemon Curd Tart

This tangy, fragrant tart is a feast for your taste buds. The tangy lemon curd and delicate coconut crust are a match made in heaven and balance each other so well.

Time: 1 1/4 hours
Servings: 8

Ingredients:
Crust:
1 1/2 cups shredded coconut
1/2 cup all-purpose flour
2 tablespoons butter, melted
1 egg white
Filling:
4 lemons, juiced and zested
5 egg yolks
4 drops stevia extract
1/2 cup butter, cubed
Topping:
1 cup heavy cream
1 drop stevia extract
1/2 teaspoon vanilla extract
Coconut flakes

Directions:
1. Preheat your oven to 350F and prepare a round tart pan.
2. For the crust, mix all the ingredients in a food processor and pulse until well combined.
3. Spoon the mixture into your prepared pan and press it well on the bottom and sides of the pan.
4. Bake in the oven for 15 minutes or until slightly golden brown.
5. For the filling, combine all the ingredients in a heatproof bowl and place the bowl in the microwave on high settings 30 seconds at a time until it begins to thicken.

6. Pour the curd into the baked crust and refrigerate until chilled and set.
7. For the topping, whip the cream until stiff. Add the stevia and vanilla and spoon the whipped cream over the lemon tart.
8. Refrigerate until the serving time.

Walnut Apple Pie

The walnut crust and crisp topping make this pie a delicacy, even though it doesn't really fall under the traditional pie category. But stepping out of your comfort zone is good sometimes, right?!

Time: 1 hour
Servings: 8-10

Ingredients:
Crust:
1 cup walnuts, ground
1/2 cup oat flour
1/2 cup dried breadcrumbs
1/4 cup butter, melted
1 pinch salt
1 egg white
Filling:
6 red apples, peeled, cored and sliced
2 tablespoons cornstarch
1/2 teaspoon cinnamon powder
1/2 teaspoon ground ginger
Topping:
1 cup almond flour
2 tablespoons cold butter

Directions:
1. Preheat your oven to 350F and prepare a round pie pan.
2. For the crust, mix all the ingredients in a food processor and pulse until well combined.
3. Spoon the mixture into your pan and press it well on the bottom and sides of the pan.
4. For the filling, mix all the ingredients in a bowl then transfer the mixture into your crust.
5. For the topping, mix the flour with butter until grainy then spread the mixture over the apples.
6. Bake in the oven for 50 minutes or until golden brown and crusty.

7. Serve the pie chilled.

Sweet Potato Pie

Sweet potato, although a vegetable, has been used in desserts with great success for years and this pie is one of those examples. Sweet potatoes have a certain natural sweetness that recommends them for sugar-free desserts. Combine them with spices and you've got yourself a delicious sweet treat.

Time: 1 1/2 hours
Servings: 8-10

Ingredients:
Crust:
1 cup pecans, ground
1 cup all-purpose flour
1/4 cup butter, chilled
2-4 tablespoons cold water
Filling:
4 sweet potatoes
1/2 teaspoon cinnamon powder
1/2 teaspoon ground ginger
4 eggs
1 pinch salt
1 teaspoon vanilla extract

Directions:
1. Preheat your oven to 350F and prepare a round pie pan.
2. For the crust, mix all the ingredients in a food processor, adding the water gradually until it comes together into a dough.
3. Transfer the dough into your prepared pan and press it well on the bottom and sides with your fingertips. Place in the fridge until needed.
4. For the filling, wrap the sweet potatoes in aluminum foil and bake them at 400F for 30 minutes.
5. Once baked, remove the skin and scoop the baked flesh into a food processor. Pulse until smooth.

6. Add the rest of the ingredients and pour the mixture into your crust.
7. Bake in the oven for 40 minutes or until the edges turn golden brown and the center looks set.
8. Remove from the oven and let the pie cool completely before slicing and serving.

Fresh Berry Mint Tart

Don't underestimate the taste of this tart. The key to a delicious tart is the crust, which given the fact that there is no additional filling but berries, has to be slightly thicker than your usual pies.

Time: 30 minutes
Servings: 8

Ingredients:
Crust:
1 cup shredded coconut
1 cup almond flour
1/4 cup cornstarch
1 egg yolk
1 pinch salt
1/2 teaspoon vanilla extract
Filling:
3 cups fresh mixed berries
2 tablespoons chopped fresh mint
2 oz. dark chocolate, melted

Directions:
1. Preheat your oven to 350F and prepare a round tart pan.
2. For the crust, mix the coconut, almond flour, cornstarch, egg yolk, salt and vanilla in a food processor and pulse until well combined.
3. Spoon the mixture into your prepared pan and spread it into the pan with your fingertips, pressing it well at the same time.
4. Bake in the oven for 15 minutes then remove from the oven and let it cool completely.
5. Once chilled, fill the crust with fresh berries. Sprinkle with chopped mint and drizzle the berries with melted chocolate.
6. Serve the tart fresh. Store it in the refrigerator in the meantime.
7. It is best served during the same day.

Sugar-Free Pear Pie

Pears are delicate and have a mild aroma which makes them great for desserts. This pie is not the traditional kind though. Instead of a double crust, the pie consists of a crust, pears and a filling based on fresh cream and vanilla so when it bakes it becomes incredibly creamy and rich.

Time: 1 hour
Servings: 8

Ingredients:
Crust:
1 cup all-purpose flour
1/4 cup ground walnuts
1 pinch salt
1/4 cup butter, chilled and cubed
2-4 tablespoons cold water
Filling:
4 ripe pears, peeled, cored and sliced
2 eggs
1 cup heavy cream
1 teaspoon vanilla extract
1 teaspoon cornstarch

Directions:
1. Preheat your oven to 350F and prepare a round pie pan.
2. To make the crust, mix all the ingredients in a food processor and pulse until well combined.
3. Transfer the dough on a floured working surface and roll it into a thin sheet.
4. Transfer the dough into your prepared pan and press it well on the bottom and sides. Trim the edges if needed.
5. For the filling, arrange the pear slices into the crust.
6. In a bowl, mix the cream vanilla and cornstarch and pour this mixture over the pears.
7. Bake in the oven for 40 minutes or until golden brown and set.

8. Allow the pie to cool completely before slicing and serving.

Peanut Butter Smooth Pie

This pie is rich and intense, smooth and creamy and it offers both taste and texture into just one tiny bite.

Time: 1 hour
Servings: 8

Ingredients:
Crust:
1 1/2 cups sugar-free cookie crumbs
4 tablespoons butter, melted
1 tablespoon peanut butter
Filling:
8 oz. low fat cream cheese
1 cup smooth peanut butter
4 drops stevia extract
1 teaspoon vanilla extract
1 1/2 cups heavy cream, whipped

Directions:
1. Preheat your oven to 350F and prepare a round pie pan.
2. For the crust, mix the ingredients in a food processor and pulse until well combined.
3. Transfer the mixture into your pie pan and press it well on the bottom and sides of the pan.
4. Bake the crust in the oven for 10-15 minutes or until golden brown. Remove from the oven when done and let it cool completely.
5. For the filling, mix the cream cheese with peanut butter, stevia and vanilla until smooth.
6. Fold in the whipped heavy cream then spoon the filling into the pie crust.
7. Refrigerate until serving.

Muffins

Banana Blueberry Muffins

Banana have a certain natural sweetness that works well in this combination, no added sugar being needed for this recipe. The blueberries are there for an extra punch of delicate flavor and color and they bring these muffins to a whole new level of deliciousness.

Time: 45 minutes
Servings: 12

Ingredients:
3 ripe bananas, mashed
1 egg
1/2 cup water
1/2 cup vegetable oil
1 cup all-purpose flour
1 cup whole wheat flour
1 pinch salt
1 teaspoon baking soda
1 pinch nutmeg
3/4 cup fresh or frozen blueberries

Directions:
1. Preheat your oven to 350F and prepare a muffin pan by lining it with muffin papers.
2. In a bowl, mix the bananas, egg, water and oil then stir in the dry ingredients.
3. With a spatula, fold in the blueberries then spoon the batter into your prepared muffin pan.
4. Bake in the oven for 20 minutes or until well risen and golden brown.
5. Allow the muffins to cool in the pan before serving.

Everything-but-the-kitchen-sink Muffins

As the name states, these muffins are a mix of everything one might have in his pantry, but the final muffins do taste like dessert with their intense flavors and delicate aroma of apples, oats and cranberries.

Time: 45 minutes
Servings: 24

Ingredients:
1 1/2 cups applesauce
2 eggs
1 teaspoon vanilla extract
1 ripe banana, mashed
3 cups rolled oats
1 cup almond flour
1/4 cup ground flaxseeds
1 1/2 teaspoon baking soda
1 teaspoon cinnamon powder
1/2 cup dried cranberries
1/4 cup raisins
1/4 cup walnuts, chopped

Directions:
1. Preheat your oven to 350F and line 2 muffin tins with muffin papers.
2. For the muffins, combine the applesauce, eggs, vanilla and bananas in a bowl.
3. Stir in the remaining ingredients and give it a good mix.
4. Spoon the batter into your prepared muffin tins and bake for 20 minutes or until golden brown.
5. Allow the muffins to cool in the pan before serving.

Sugar-Free Pumpkin Muffins

Slightly spiced and moist, these muffins are tiny gems of deliciousness. You would never expect a sugar-free dessert to taste so good, but they do!

Time: 45 minutes
Servings: 12

Ingredients:
1 cup whole wheat flour
1 cup all-purpose flour
1 1/2 teaspoons baking powder
1/2 teaspoon cinnamon powder
1/2 teaspoon ground ginger
1 pinch salt
1 cup pumpkin puree
1/2 cup applesauce
2 eggs
1/4 cup vegetable oil
1/2 cup walnuts, chopped

Directions:
1. Preheat your oven to 350F and line a muffin tin with muffin papers. Place aside.
2. Combine the flours with baking powder, cinnamon, ginger and salt in a bowl.
3. Add the remaining ingredients and give it a quick mix. Don't over-mix the batter as it changes the texture. A few lumps in the batter are ok.
4. Spoon the batter into your prepared muffin tin and bake in the oven for 20 minutes or until golden brown and well risen.
5. Allow the muffins to cool completely before serving.

Raspberry Whole Wheat Muffins

Using whole wheat flour and fresh raspberries, these muffins are refreshing and delicious. Their aroma is delicate and their fiber content is high and that makes them perfect for kids' snacks at any time of the day.

Time: 40 minutes
Servings: 12

Ingredients:
2 cups whole wheat flour
1 teaspoon baking powder
1 pinch salt
2 eggs
2/3 cup heavy cream
1/2 teaspoon vanilla extract
1 cup fresh raspberries

Directions:
1. Preheat the oven to 350F and line a muffin tin with special muffin papers.
2. Mix the flour, baking powder and salt in a bowl.
3. In a different bowl, combine the eggs with the heavy cream and mix well.
4. Stir in the flour then fold in the raspberries.
5. Spoon the batter into your prepared muffin tin and bake in the oven for 20-25 minutes or until well risen and golden brown.
6. Allow the muffins to cool completely in the pan before serving.
7. Store the muffins in an airtight container for up to 4 days.

Banana Peanut Butter Muffins

Peanut butter and bananas are a classic combination that tastes heavenly for any peanut butter lover out there. And who wouldn't love a delicious, moist treat after all?!

Time: 40 minutes
Servings: 12

Ingredients:
3 ripe bananas, mashed
1/2 cup smooth peanut butter
1/2 cup low fat yogurt
1 egg
1/4 cup vegetable oil
1 teaspoon vanilla extract
1 cup all-purpose flour
1/2 cup whole wheat flour
1 pinch salt
1 teaspoon baking powder
1/2 teaspoon baking soda
1/2 teaspoon cinnamon powder

Directions:
1. Combine the bananas, peanut butter, yogurt, egg, oil and vanilla in a food processor and pulse until smooth.
2. Stir in the flours, salt, baking powder, baking soda and cinnamon and pulse just until well mixed.
3. Spoon the batter into 12 muffin cups lined with muffin papers.
4. Bake in the preheated oven at 350F for 20 minutes or until fragrant and well risen.
5. Allow the muffins to cool in the pan before serving them or storing them away.

Sugar-Free Carrot Muffins

Similar with the classic carrot cake, these muffins rely on the natural sweetness and aroma of carrots and dates to make this dessert sweet. But those two ingredients make more than that – they also delicately flavor the muffins and turn them into a real treat.

Time: 45 minutes
Servings: 18

Ingredients:
1 cup sweet rice flour
1 cup almond flour
2 teaspoons baking soda
1/2 teaspoon cinnamon powder
1 pinch salt
1 cup dates, pitted
3 eggs
3 ripe bananas
1/4 cup coconut oil
1 cup grated carrot
1/4 cup walnuts, chopped

Directions:
1. Preheat your oven to 350F and prepare your muffin tin or cups by lining them with special muffin papers.
2. Combine the dates and eggs in a food processor and pulse until smooth.
3. Stir in the bananas and coconut oil and mix well.
4. Stir in the remaining ingredients then pour the batter into your muffin cups, filling them only 3/4 as they will rise.
5. Bake in the preheated oven for 20-25 minutes or until fragrant and golden brown.
6. Allow the muffins to cool in the pan before serving or storing in an airtight container.

Nectarine Pecan Muffins

Similar to peaches, nectarines are easily found all year around so you can make these muffins when your sweet tooth goes crazy.

Time: 45 minutes
Servings: 12

Ingredients:
1 1/2 cups whole wheat flour
1/2 cup all-purpose flour
1 teaspoon baking powder
1/2 teaspoon baking soda
1 pinch salt
1/4 cup vegetable oil
1/2 cup almond milk
4 drops stevia extract
2 eggs
1/2 teaspoon vanilla extract
3 ripe peaches, pitted and diced
1/2 cup pecans, chopped

Directions:
1. Preheat your oven to 350F and line a muffin tin with special muffin papers.
2. Combine the flours, baking powder, baking soda and salt in a bowl.
3. Stir in the oil, almond milk, stevia and eggs, as well as vanilla. Give it a quick mix then fold in the peaches and pecans.
4. Spoon the batter into your muffin cups, filling them only 3/4 as they tend to rise.
5. Bake in the oven for 25 minutes or until fragrant and golden brown, as well as well risen.
6. When done, remove from the oven and let them cool on a wire rack.

Plum Bran Muffins

Bran is known as being loaded with fibers. In addition to this, it is also an ingredient that has a special taste of its own which is rather earthy so it combines well with stone fruit fruits, including plums, peaches or apricots.

Time: 45 minutes
Servings: 12

Ingredients:
1 cup unprocessed wheat bran
1 cup all-purpose flour
1 pinch salt
1/4 teaspoon cinnamon powder
1 teaspoon baking powder
1/4 teaspoon baking soda
1/2 cup almond milk
1/2 cup plain yogurt
1 egg
1/2 teaspoon vanilla extract
6 ripe plums, pitted and diced

Directions:
1. Preheat your oven to 350F and line a muffin tin with special muffin papers. Place the tin aside until you'll need it.
2. Combine the bran with flour, salt, cinnamon, baking powder and baking soda in a bowl.
3. In a different bowl mix the almond milk, yogurt, egg and vanilla and mix well.
4. Pour this mixture over the bran and give it a quick mix.
5. Fold in the plums then spoon the batter into your prepared muffin tin.
6. Bake for 20-25 minutes or until golden brown and well risen.
7. When done, remove them from the oven and let them cool in the pan before serving.
8. Store the muffins in an airtight container for up to 4 days, if they last that long.

Zucchini Quinoa Muffins

Quinoa is known as the super-grain of the future due to its amazing health benefits and high nutritional profile which includes vitamins, fibers and minerals, more of these nutrients than any other grain. It's an ingredient that tastes great in savory foods, but it does just as good in desserts, these muffins being the proof of that.

Time: 40 minutes
Servings: 18

Ingredients:
1 cup whole wheat flour
1 cup all-purpose flour
1 teaspoon baking powder
1 teaspoon baking soda
1 pinch salt
1/4 teaspoon cinnamon powder
2 young zucchinis, grated
1 cup cooked quinoa
1 ripe banana, mashed
3 eggs
1/2 teaspoon vanilla extract

Directions:
1. Preheat your oven to 350F and prepare your muffin cups by lining it with special muffin papers.
2. Combine the flours with baking powder, baking soda, salt and cinnamon in a bowl.
3. In a different bowl, mix the zucchinis, quinoa, banana, eggs and vanilla.
4. Stir in the dry ingredients you mixed earlier and give it a quick mix.
5. Spoon the batter into your prepared muffin cups, filling them only 3/4 way through.
6. Bake in the oven for 25 minutes or until well risen and golden brown on top.

7. Allow the muffins to cool in the cups before serving and store them for up to 4 days.

Chocolate Zucchini Muffins

Although surprising, the mix between chocolate and zucchinis feels the most natural thing once you taste these muffins. The explanation is the fact that zucchinis simply don't have a flavor of their own so the chocolate is the one that stands out in this recipe.

Time: 45 minutes
Servings: 12

Ingredients:
1 1/2 cups whole wheat flour
1/4 cup dark cocoa powder
1 teaspoon baking soda
1 pinch salt
1 pinch nutmeg
1/4 teaspoon cinnamon powder
1/4 cup vegetable oil
4 drops stevia extract
2 eggs
1 young zucchini, grated
1/2 cup almond milk
1/2 cup pecans, chopped

Directions:
1. Preheat your oven to 350F and line your muffin cups with muffin papers.
2. Combine the flour, cocoa powder, baking soda, salt, nutmeg and cinnamon in a bowl.
3. Stir in the remaining ingredients and give it a quick mix with a spoon.
4. Pour the batter into your muffin cups, filling them only 3/4 way through as they tend to rise.
5. Bake in the oven at 350F for 20 minutes or until the muffins pass the toothpick test – insert a toothpick in the center of one muffin; if it comes out clean, they are done but if it still has traces of batter, bake a few more minutes then check again.

6. Allow the muffins to cool in their cups before serving.
7. Store them no longer than 5 days.

Conclusion

A sugar-free diet simply means taking your carb intake from elsewhere – fresh fruits, nuts, oats, vegetables and healthy ingredients. It's not a diet that has as main purpose losing weight or achieving any goal other than recalibrate your body and improve your body's functions by feeding it with healthy food, loaded with fibers and vitamins, thus considerably reducing the risk of developing diabetes, becoming obese or having serious heart problems.

It's not a damaging diet, but one that enriches your lifestyle and improves your digestion, your nutrient absorption and your general health over all. However, do keep in mind that it's not an easy diet, especially in the first days when your cravings might occur more and more frequently. But don't give up! Stay strong and only snack on sugar-free desserts whenever your sweet tooth goes crazy. The result is well worth the effort, trust my words!

Printed in Great Britain
by Amazon

44996127R00040